For the Love of the Game

Michael Jordan and Me

by Eloise Greenfield

Illustrations by Jan Spivey Gilchrist

HarperCollinsPublishers

Special thanks to models
Camille Elly and William K. Gilchrist

For the Love of the Game
Michael Jordan and Me
Text copyright © 1997 by Eloise Greenfield
Illustrations copyright © 1997 by Jan Spivey Gilchrist
Printed in the U.S.A. All rights reserved.

Library of Congress Cataloging-in-Publication Data
Greenfield, Eloise.
   For the love of the game : Michael Jordan and me / by Eloise Greenfield ;
illustrated by Jan Spivey Gilchrist.
      p.   cm.
   Summary: Two children discover the importance of the human spirit and
recognize their similarity to basketball star Michael Jordan.
   ISBN 0-06-027298-8. — ISBN 0-06-027299-6 (lib. bdg.)
   1. Jordan, Michael, 1963–   —Juvenile poetry.   2. Basketball players—
United States—Juvenile poetry.   3. Children's poetry, American.   [1. Self-
realization—Poetry.   2. Jordan, Michael, 1963–   —Poetry.   3. American
poetry.]   I. Gilchrist, Jan Spivey, ill.   II. Title.
PS3557.R39416F67   1997   95-51655
811'.54—dc20   CIP
                                                                                AC

Typography by Nancy Sabato
2   3   4   5   6   7   8   9   10
❖

To children, with love
It is our fervent hope that this book will
inspire you to see your own strength,
discover and develop your talents (*everyone* has them!)
and move always toward health and growth
and happiness.

Eloise Greenfield and Jan Spivey Gilchrist

When he was just a little boy
when he was just a kid
Michael saw a basketball
and *this* is what he did . . .

FROM NORTH CAROLINA,

AT GUARD, SIX-SIX,

MI - CHAEL JORDAN!

For the love of the game

he rises from the chair

he steps to the court
he greets his team
he takes his stance
he makes his move

he slaps the ball
from clutching hands
snaps it to a friend
helps his team to win
he forgets to obey
the law of gravity
jumps not up and down
but up and up
and up, then *stops*

stands right there
on a little piece of air
will he shoot from the left
or shoot from the right?
which hand will he use tonight?
he sails higher, holds the ball
above the bucket, and *slam!*
jams it through the net

before he lands, smooth

as a gliding plane, then

turns and smiles

at the memory of flying.

For the love of the game
of life

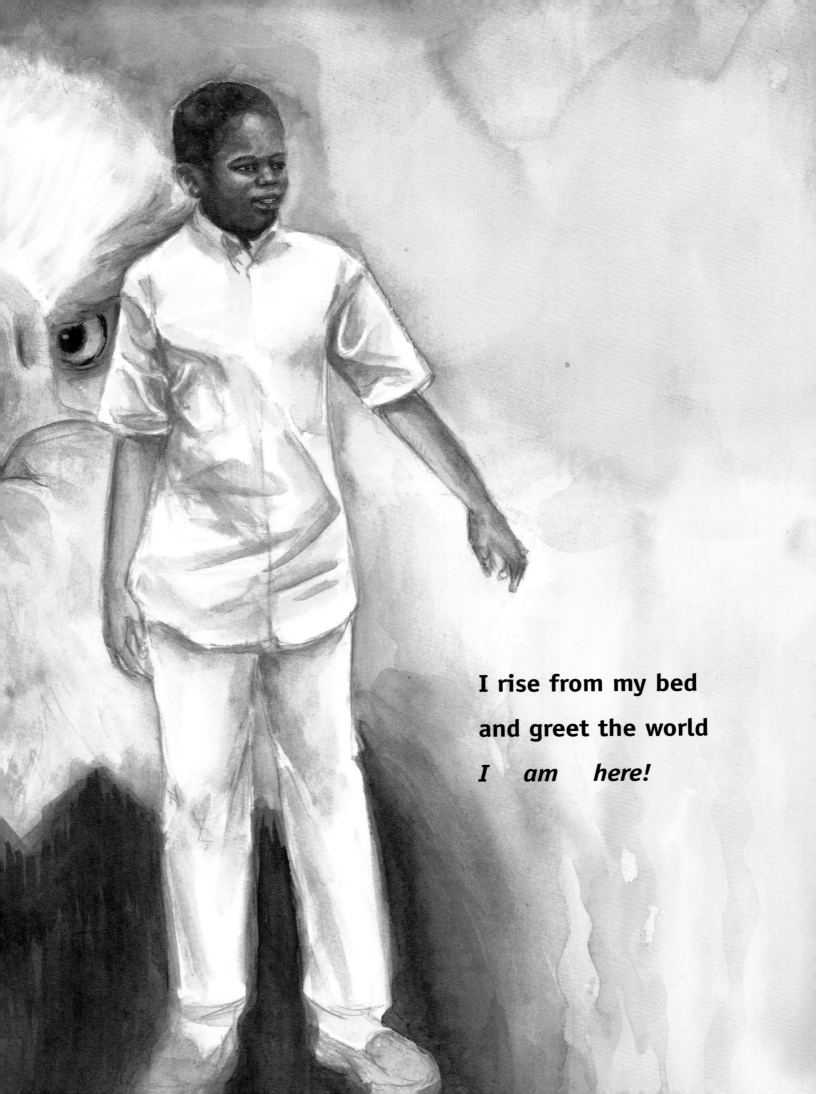

I rise from my bed
and greet the world
I   am   here!

The sun has risen

but barely

in the pale light

I see a world of many paths

partly hidden by trees

and shadows of trees

it is a puzzle

of power and beauty

and I must see more

someday I will choose a path

and go

But I hear the voices
of naysayers
You can't, too hard,
you can't

I hear the voices

of doomsayers

Danger! All is danger!

and I am afraid

under what tree lie the roots

that will trip me?

in which shadow hide the holes

that will swallow me?

Then through the din of voices

I hear the chanting of people

who love me

If you fall you will

rise again

I breathe their words
I feel the strength
of my spirit
if I fall I will rise again
the sun is at midmorning
the time to prepare
is now.

In the game of life

I choose to choose

the path that I will take

I listen to my heart

beating *my* rhythm

I take my stance

I make my move.

For the love of the game

of my life

I live.